It has been a pleasure to have led this expedition and created such a beautiful product that will prolong the stories of these inspirational individuals from both the local Doncaster community and the United Kingdom as a whole. I would like to thank all of the experts that have been used within our expedition as without their stories, this book would not exist and the children would not have had the same impactful experiences they have had. Your stories have helped them to reflect on the varied experiences of men, women and children during the Second World War and allowed them hear first-hand, the way in which war can change somebody's life profoundly. The stories we have heard have made us realise just how lucky we are to not have to go through the same things that they did all those years ago.

I must also say a big well done to all of the children within Year 3 and 4. You have shown incredible enthusiasm for this expedition and produced some fantastic work that you can all be proud of. Whether it has been your biography writing, your moving war poetry or some of the incredible monoprint artwork, you have all worked extremely hard to make this product the best version it could possibly be.

After reading their writing and speaking to the children on a daily basis, I am confident that every child within Year 3 and 4 could answer our guiding question and explain some of the ways in which war can change a person's life.

Jake Taylor
Expedition Coordinator
Green Top School

LEST WE FORGET
HOW DOES WAR CHANGE LIVES?

In September 2022, Year 3 and 4 began their Learning Expedition focusing on World War Two. It was called 'Lest We Forget' and the guiding question was 'How does war change lives?'

The Learning Targets were:

History

I can describe different accounts of a historical event.

I can suggest causes and consequences of some of the main events in history.

I can use dates and terms to describe events.

I can describe the character experiences of eristic features of the past, including ideas, beliefs, attitudes and experiences of men, women and children.

Art

I can create a sketch book to record my observations and use them to review and revisit ideas.

I can demonstrate a mastery understanding of art and design techniques, including drawing, painting and sculpture with a range of materials; for example, pencil, charcoal, paint, clay.

I can discuss and compare the work of great artists, architects and designers in history.

Our Learning

We looked at history in depth to enable us to build a strong knowledge of World War Two. We studied evacuation, The Blitz, the roles of men, women and children in the war, and rationing.

To drive our English in Case Study 1, we used the text, 'The Lion and the Unicorn' which linked closely to our learning on evacuees. We focused on letter writing within English, which was heavily driven by our learning within the expedition. We also used a wide-range of non-fiction texts to support our understanding and build our background knowledge.

For Case Study 2, we continued to use a range of non-fiction texts to support our writing, particularly biographies as this was our main writing focus. We looked at the biographies of heroes from the Second World War, especially those covering the roles of women or others who made a significant contribution to the outcome of the war. We then used our learning to write biographies about experts, whose stories made up part of our final product.

During Case Study 3, we turned our focus to art and creating monoprint portraits of our experts. We looked at a range of different sketching techniques which we then used to create an initial sketch of our experts. We then critiqued our work before creating a final draft which was then used to create our monoprints. In addition to this, our English lessons focused on war poetry and the powerful message that it can convey. We looked at several famous wartime poems and these helped to inspire us to write our own poems. As a phase, we created a range of acrostic poems, haikus and tankas that linked to a different aspect of the war. These would again go on to make up part of our final product.

Hooks, Learning Visits and Environments

The children were hooked into their learning through building background knowledge, immersion days and experience days. The building of background knowledge ensured equity for all at the start of the expedition.

They were hooked into the learning by looking at wartime artefacts such as helmets, gas masks and other memorabilia from the time during one of our lessons. Immersive activities included creating spitfire planes, making gas mask boxes and creating 'Blitz' artwork. 'Family Learning' also took place during our first case study, which focused on immersing the classroom environment through the creation of Anderson Shelters. War radio clips, air raid sirens and wartime music was also played at various points to help immerse both the parents and children into the session. Experience days included a visit to the local church to recreate an evacuation, as well as a visit to Eden Camp to further develop our background knowledge.

Assessment

Our significant assessment pieces for this expedition were letter writing, biography writing and poetry. We produced multiple drafts which were edited and improved throughout the cycle. We also produced monoprint artwork to showcase our sketching skills which have been built up during the case study. Again, these were drafted and critiqued multiple times before producing the final outcome.

Final Product

The expedition culminated in the creation of a book to celebrate the stories of local community members who were alive during the Second World War.

In addition to those, we also looked at some well-known people who also played a key role in the outcome of the war. We were able to hear stories of both soldiers who were caught up in the fighting as well as those who were just children at the time, offering a wide-range of experiences for the children to reflect upon. The book was made up of biographies, poems and artwork.

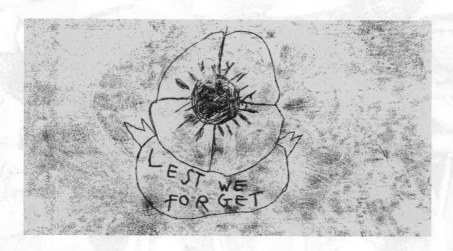

Contents

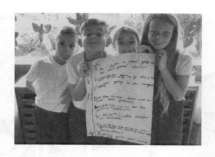

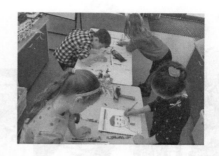

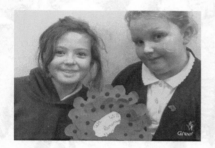

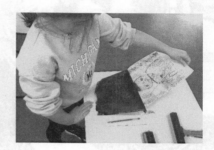

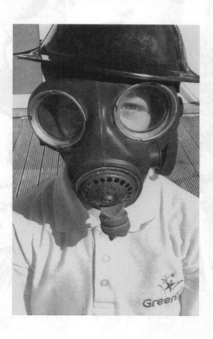

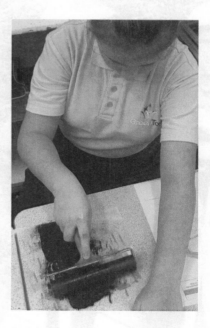

HARRY
HEWITT

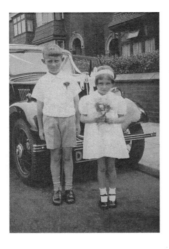

Early life

Harry was born in 1930, in a town called Balby in the city of Doncaster. When he was young, he lived with his aunt, uncle and one of his cousins called Sid. Harry was nine when World War Two broke out. He had a couple of hobbies when he was a young boy. He enjoyed collecting extremely rare and interesting stamps. He also loved spending time making and building model aircraft in his spare time. At the age of ten he joined the army cadets, which he enjoyed.

Jobs in the war

Harry, as a child, had a few jobs which helped support the war effort at home on the homefront. One of the jobs he had as an army cadet was a runner. This meant he had to run through Balby, Hexthorpe and Sprotbrough delivering important messages between the home guards. Another job Harry had, was a job he and many others had at school. This was a salvage monitor. As a salvage monitor, Harry would collect scrap metal, aluminium tins, glass bottles and newspapers. These items would be weighed, cleaned, reused and recycled. Some of it would also have been used to help repair planes and tanks.

While the war was going on, Harry grew his own vegetables. As well as this he would also catch butterflies for a penny a week, usually in glass jars. This helped keep his and other people's crops safe as the butterflies would usually lay their eggs on the plants and then the caterpillars would eat and destroy them. Doing this meant Harry and his family had more food to eat and share between them.

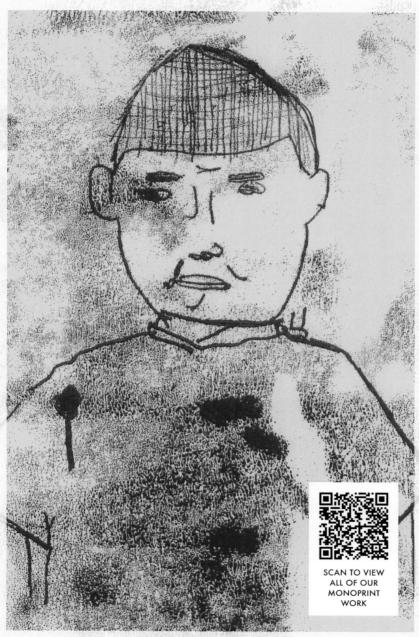

SCAN TO VIEW
ALL OF OUR
MONOPRINT
WORK

ARTIST Reuben R

School during the war

School wasn't what it used to be before the war. Harry said he grew scared of the air raids when they would happen. He said this was because of all the practising they would do at school. He used to have to practise putting on his gas mask and practise getting to the air raid shelter in the school grounds daily, which left him feeling very nervous of when the Germans would attack. This meant that Harry used to miss a lot of school time and learning with all this practice. Also, if the air raid siren had gone off for real the day before, this meant that they would not be expected to attend school the next day either.

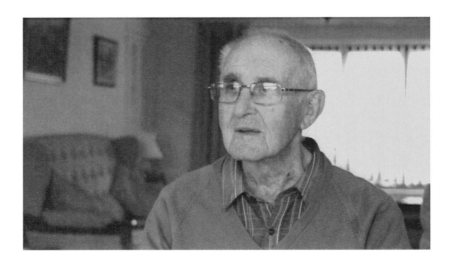

AUTHORS

Early life: Rowan T, Sonny G, Alfie F, Marshall P.
Jobs in the war: Carter A, Gabriella H, Maya K, Letti B, Isaac B.
School during the war: Samantha W Elizabeth S, Sonny G, Ellie-Mai S.

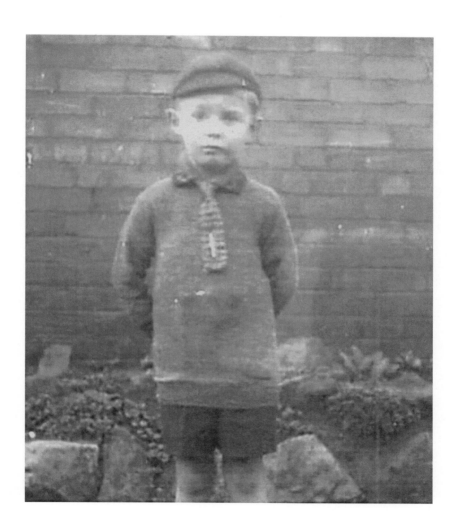

BOB & BETTY
SALTER

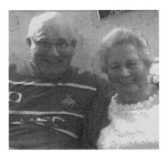

Early life

Bob and Betty Salter were both born in Doncaster and experienced their childhood during the height of World War II. Bob's full name is John Robert Salter and was seven years old, living in Barnby Dun. Betty was four when the war began and lived in Edlington.

Life during the war

During the war, both had lots of worries filling their heads. Betty was most worried about the doodlebugs (huge metal bombs with large wings) filling the sky above her house whereas Bob spent his days worrying about the loud air raid sirens and also his aunt coming to stay. He remembers his house being very crowded during this time, making daily life very difficult.

Betty recalls a big, wooden table in her house which came in useful when the air raid sirens went off. As clear as day, Betty remembers hearing the terrifyingly loud sound and running to find shelter, and safety, under this table.

School during the war

At school, Bob remembers being told that if the air raid siren did go off and you lived more than 5 minutes away from school, you would have to stay at school until it was safe to leave. However, if you lived less than 5 minutes away, you were able to run home quickly to seek shelter.

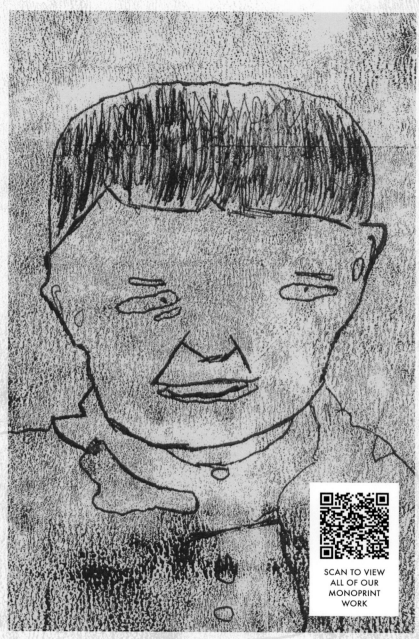

SCAN TO VIEW
ALL OF OUR
MONOPRINT
WORK

ARTIST Jobey G

Rationing

As children, both Bob and Betty recall having a ration book and not being able to get things as easily such as sugared foods and also fruit as you couldn't get these in from different countries due to the war. They both said it was difficult as they were partial to a sweet treat (and still are)!

It was a time that, as a nation, everyone had to pull together. Generously, Betty's mother spent her time supporting where she could and was known for her talents with a needle and thread. Betty remembers her mum changing adult clothes into children's clothes for people in the local community so that nobody was left without.

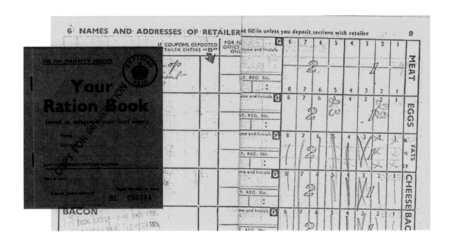

AUTHORS

Early life: Isla D, Bobby T, Esmae W.
Life during the war: Hollie H, Benjamin R-W, George H-B, Isla H, Natalia P, Cohen S, Aidan W.
School during the war: Francesca S, Reuben P, Katie M.
Rationing: Marnie-Rose E, Teddy A, Heidi H, Layra R, Reef R, Heidi R, Jobey G.

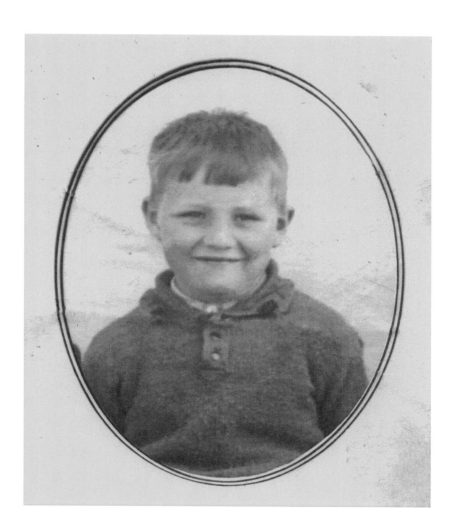

JOHN BURNS

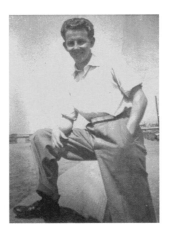

Early life

John Burns, who is currently 92 years old, grew up during World War II and has lots of interesting memories. John was born 3rd September 1930 in Doncaster. Sadly, on his ninth birthday, he had got back from church and was at his grandmother's house when he heard on the radio that World War II had been declared. However, nothing really changed for him as it was about a year before the war really started to get going in Britain.

Life during the war

One of the things that John remembers from the war is rationing. John grew up in a poor family so surprisingly, he actually had more food through rationing and using coupons because it was cheaper. He also thought that rationing was better for children because it was healthier than the foods we eat today. John would queue up in Doncaster in a long line just to get food parcels without knowing what was in them. He also traded on the 'black market' because he didn't have much money and sometimes traded wine for food! Sadly, since they had a very small garden and because his dad worked long hours at the mine, they didn't have time for an allotment to grow their own food.

As well as rationing, John also remembers other precautions that he and his family had to go through. Outside his house, he had a shelter in his garden which was made of brick but he never felt the need to use it because the planes bombed industrial areas and there wasn't much in Rossington worth bombing. John's school also had an air raid shelter in the rose gardens.

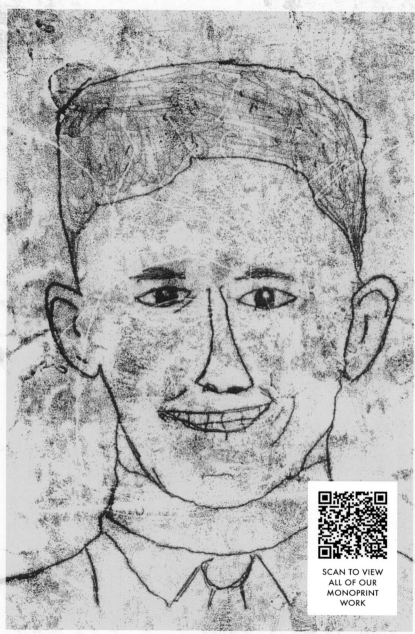

SCAN TO VIEW
ALL OF OUR
MONOPRINT
WORK

ARTIST Thea W

Interestingly, his dad volunteered as an ARP warden and helped to protect the people in Rossington. He also remembers the evacuees which came to Rossington, getting off the train with gas masks and name tags. John's family could not take any evacuees because the house was already too full of people but his grandmother did. However some of the evacuees went to John's school and he did make friends with them.

One of John's favourite memories of the war is about his sister. Before his sister had returned from a Sunday church service, a bomb had landed at the end of the street and everyone had to be evacuated. When John's sister returned home, she saw an empty street and wondered where everyone was! Luckily she saw a policeman who had to ask what she was doing there!

There were times when planes would crash to the ground and once a plane crashed close by. The children in the neighbourhood (including John) would salvage bits of material such as wire and perspex and use the bits they collected to make jewellery. Also, when Sheffield was being bombed, the sky would light up and you could see it from Rossington.

End of the war

Once World War II had ended, John attended a party in his street where over 200 people were celebrating the end of the war. He also remembers lots of people crowding around Doncaster's Mansion House for no reason other than they could! People were enjoying their freedom with no restrictions such as blackouts or air raid sirens.

Things didn't change that much after the war had finished because of things such as rationing, which was still alive for many years to come. John remembers that rationing lasted for another nine years after the war and that sweets were the last thing to come off of rationing!

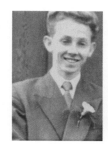
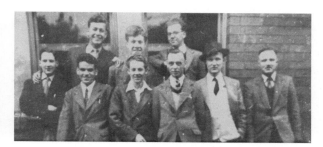

BEFORE HIS SISTER HAD RETURNED FROM A SUNDAY CHURCH SERVICE, A BOMB HAD LANDED AT THE END OF THE STREET AND EVERYONE HAD TO BE EVACUATED. WHEN JOHN'S SISTER RETURNED HOME, SHE SAW AN EMPTY STREET AND WONDERED WHERE EVERYONE WAS!

AUTHORS

Early life: Cohen P, Annis G.
Life during the war: Etta T, Annis G, Sofia B-R, Cody T-J, Victoria S, Elise W, Robyn H, Mikey G.
End of the war: Victoria S.

THOMAS
PARKINSON

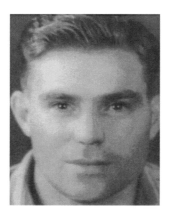

Early life

Thomas Parkinson was born on 7th November 1919 on a farm in Thorne, near Doncaster. His parents were called Herbert and Edith and he also had two brothers and five sisters. As a child, Tom didn't really enjoy school and would often struggle with reading and writing. He was, however, very good with numbers and would often use his skills when working on the farm.

Adult life

During his early adult life, Tom started working as a dustbin man before spending many years working on farms, threshing the fields and operating the tractors. It was at this time that he met his future wife, Ethel, who he would go on to marry in the midst of the Second World War. As a farmer, Tom was exempt from joining the army as farming was considered an essential job at the time. However, following a mix-up, Tom received his papers calling him up to the armed forces. Although Tom could appeal this and avoid the fighting, in his mind he felt a sense of duty to go ahead and join, having been sent the papers in the first place.

Life during the Second World War

When Tom was in the army, his brothers carried on farming and his sisters and wife went into war service. Because of his experience driving tractors, Tom spent a lot of time learning to drive lorries and armoured tanks. He was also very good with machinery and was able to fix anything that had broken down.

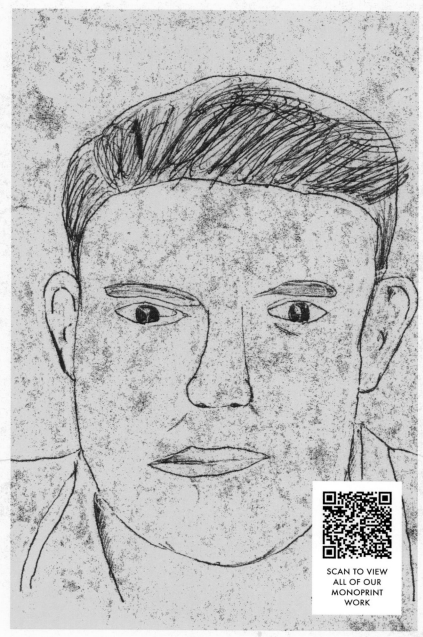

SCAN TO VIEW
ALL OF OUR
MONOPRINT
WORK

ARTIST Naomi A

When his battalion visited Doncaster, Tom and a fellow soldier took a motorbike and drove to visit his wife, who was pregnant at the time. Despite this, he would not see his daughter until she was two years old because of the war.

Tom was involved in the D-Day landings. He was part of a convoy of vehicles that landed on the beaches of Normandy on the second day of the invasion. Once he had transported the tanks, he spent much of his remaining time in the army driving them, being involved in several different battles. Tom also helped to liberate a number of Nazi concentration camps across different parts of Europe.

Following the surrender of Germany on 8th May 1945, Tom expected to return back home to Britain. However, he was later transferred to parts of Asia such as Singapore and Hong Kong, where British soldiers continued to fight the Japanese army. Due to his bravery, Tom was also asked to carry out several undercover operations before finally returning home following Japan's surrender.

Life after the war

Following the end of the Second World War, Tom returned to life as a farmer. He loved his job and did it for the rest of his working life. In 1968, he had a son as well as going on to have four grandchildren and three great-grandchildren, before sadly passing away in 2005 at the age of 85. Despite surviving the war and avoiding serious injury, Tom remained very reluctant to talk about many of the things he experienced during the Second World War.

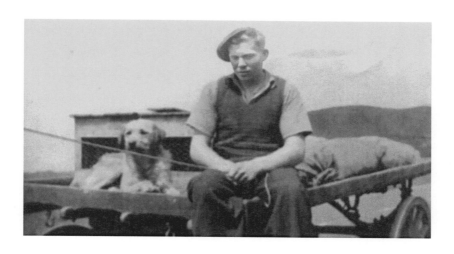

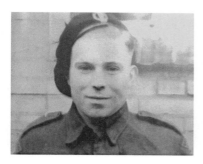

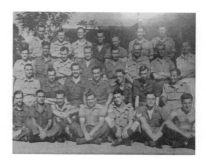

AUTHORS

Early life: Archie L, Millie P.
Adult life: Naomi A, Blake F, Chloe G.
Life during the Second World War: Harry C, Naomi A, Tobias M, Emma C, Grace Hu, Erin P.
Life after the war: Millie P, Chloe G.

AUDREY
DOCKERAY

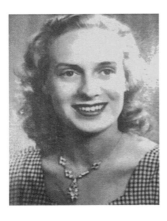

Early life

Audrey Simpson was born on 6th July 1926 in Hattersley, which is a suburb of Manchester. This was the same year that Queen Elizabeth II was born. Audrey was the second oldest out of ten children and because she was the oldest girl, she was her dad's favourite and he would often take her with him to run errands. As a child, Audrey loved going to school and learning new things.

She loved painting, reading and sewing the most. When she was twelve years old, her mum took her out of school to help out at home. This was so that she could help out with the younger children and the housework whilst her mum looked after her granny who lived at the top of the street.

Life during the war

Audrey was thirteen years old when the Second World War started but she did not need to be evacuated because her family lived on the edge of Manchester and not in the city centre. Shortly after the outbreak of war, Audrey got a job in a factory in Manchester to help out with the war effort. Her job was to boil soldiers' socks sent over from the front line, scrub them clean and then darn them, which means repairing them by sewing them up since clothes were still rationed at the time.

During the war, Audrey got scarlet fever and had to spend a few weeks in hospital. She had to stay in a ward with all different kinds of people. There were old men, women and even her dad! Because she was the only child, the other adults on the ward used to make her climb up a ladder to the skylight at night to watch the war planes flying overhead.

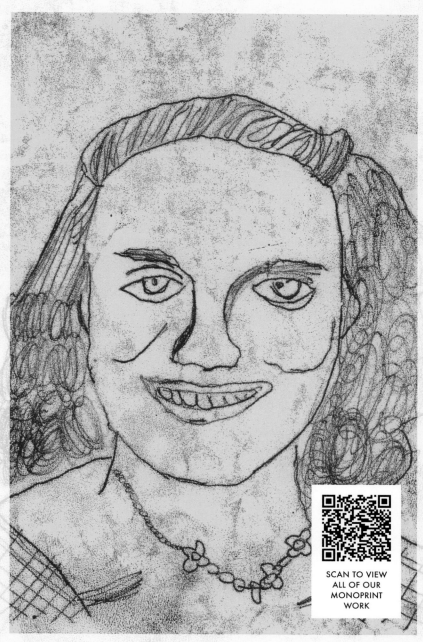

SCAN TO VIEW
ALL OF OUR
MONOPRINT
WORK

ARTIST Jersey M

At home, because sugar was rationed, treats in Audrey's house were quite rare. One cold Friday evening, her dad came home from work with a bag of boiled sweets. Audrey was so excited that she pulled the sweet from the bag and unwrapped it as fast as she could. In her excitement, she actually threw it into the fire and put the wrapper into her mouth. Sadly, she had to wait two weeks before she could have anything sweet again.

One wet evening, the air raid sirens went off and everybody had to go out to the end of the garden to the Anderson Shelter. Audrey was the last one to go towards the shelter. Because she was the last, she started running and slipped, banging her head on the floor and knocking herself out. When she woke up, nobody inside the shelter even noticed she was missing!

Life after the war

When the war finished, Audrey was nineteen years old and she had missed a lot of her school education. However, she was desperate to go back to school and catch up on her education. She applied for college and worked very hard to get the grades she needed to become a teacher.

While studying, she met a man called John Dockeray, who turned out to be the love of her life. They would later get married in 1955 and go on to have two beautiful daughters called Heather and Helen. Unfortunately, tragedy struck soon after Helen was born when John died suddenly. Despite this, she went on to live a long and happy life, having grandchildren and great-grandchildren. Audrey sadly died on 6th December 2019, but managed to live to the age of 93 years old.

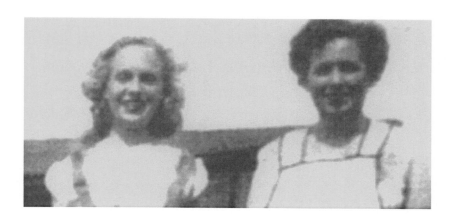

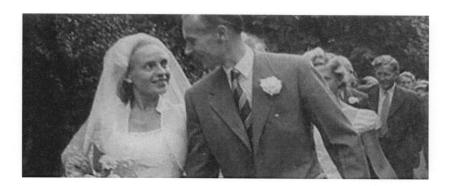

AUTHORS

Early life: Sophie K, Esme P, Ashton F, April-Grace F, Charlie T.
Life during the war: Jersey M, Emilea R, Sophie K.
Life after the war: Jersey M, Sophie K, Ryla L, Emilea R.

EILEEN
NEARNE

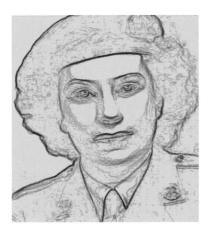

Early life

Eileen was originally born in London in 1921 and lived with her mother, father and her three other siblings. Just before the war, her family moved to France which meant she was fluent in speaking the French language. In May 1941, when the Germans invaded France, Eileen and her sister moved back to England by travelling through Spain, arriving in London in 1942.

The life of a spy: Part 1

Initially, she was offered a role in the Women's Auxiliary Air Force, probably because she was fluent in French, but she declined it. Eileen soon started working for the 'SOE' (Special Operations Executive) along with her brother and also her sister. This organisation was known as Churchill's Secret Army. To begin with, Eileen was a London based signals operator and worked in secret to sabotage missions in enemy territories.

The life of a spy: Part 2

Eileen's code name was Rose and had a few close calls with the Nazis. However, she was always one step ahead of the enemy. Proudly, Eileen sent over 105 messages to London during her mission known as 'The Wizard' where she arranged finance for the French Resistance.

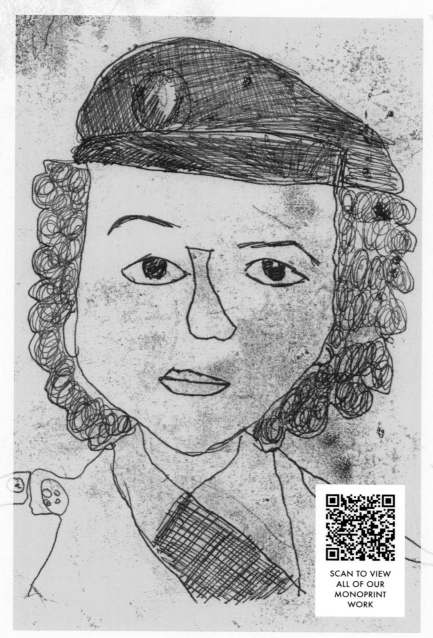

SCAN TO VIEW
ALL OF OUR
MONOPRINT
WORK

ARTIST Francesca S

Being captured

Unfortunately, Eileen was captured by the Gestapo (undercover German police). As they banged angrily on her door, she had to work quickly to burn the evidence such as her messages and hide the transmitter but they did find her radio and coding pad. During her time with the Gestapo, she was treated horribly and was beaten very badly.

Women's concentration camp

In 1944, Eileen had her head shaved when she was a prisoner in Ravensbruck concentration camp. Sadly, she was tortured, but she never told the truth of who she really was as she was concerned about her SOE colleagues and their safety after she was captured. In total, Eileen moved around several different labour camps where she had to work very long days. One evening, on a night time march, she seized her opportunity to escape along with two other prisoners where they spent many days without food. Luckily, the three women were hidden safely away in a church by a priest.

After the war

After the war, Eileen Nearne (when she finally came back to England) was in a state of physical and emotional lockdown because of the war. She never managed to gain employment in a job as the war had left her badly traumatised and people stopped remembering her. She lived a peaceful, quiet life in Torquay, along with her sister until she died in 2010. Finally, as her life was uncovered, she was given a funeral with full military honours that celebrated her achievements and her service to her country.

IN 1944, EILEEN HAD HER HEAD SHAVED WHEN SHE WAS A PRISONER IN RAVENSBRUCK CONCENTRATION CAMP. SADLY, SHE WAS TORTURED, BUT SHE NEVER TOLD THE TRUTH OF WHO SHE REALLY WAS AS SHE WAS CONCERNED ABOUT HER SOE COLLEAGUES AND THEIR SAFETY AFTER SHE WAS CAPTURED.

AUTHORS

Early life: Isla D, Reuben P, Jobey G, Lara S.
The life of a spy - Part 1: Teddy A, Hollie H, Heidi H, George H-B.
The life of a spy - Part 2: Marnie-Rose E, Katie M, Layla R, Benjamin R-W.
Being captured: Reef R, Andrew K, Bobby T, Natalia P.
Women's concentration camp: Francesca S, Heidi R, Esmae W.
After the war: Aidan W, Isla H, Cohen S.

SIR DOUGLAS
BADER

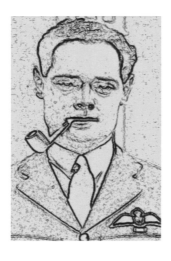

Early life

Douglas Bader was born in London in 1910. His dad was a soldier in World War I but he died from a shrapnel injury.
His mum eventually remarried and the family moved to Sprotbrough, near Doncaster. Douglas went to school in Oxford and also went to RAF College.
He was good at sport and captained the Rugby team and was a champion boxer. When Douglas was a little boy, he loved the fighter aces and this made him want to be a pilot one day.

Before the war

In 1930, Douglas graduated as a pilot officer. A year later, he was selected to fly in the elite RAF aerobatic team. They would perform stunts and do aerial displays.

On 14th December 1931, solo flying, he was performing one of his specialities – slow rolls at very low altitude – in his British Bulldog fighter. His left wing clipped the ground and he crashed. Miraculously, he was not killed! His right leg, however, was amputated that night and his left leg a few days later. Douglas' determination enabled him to learn to walk again. As a consequence of the accident, Douglas was discharged from the RAF. He found work with the Asiatic Petroleum Company. He thought this job was boring and it made him feel unhappy and depressed.

In this time, Douglas met and married Thelma Edwards in 1935. When World War II started, he got the chance to take up his first love, flying, again.

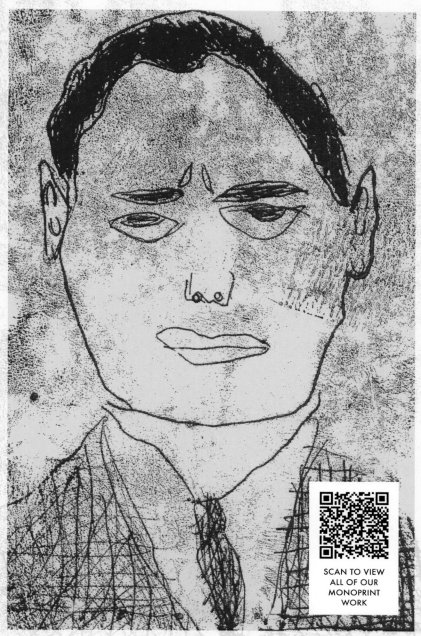

SCAN TO VIEW
ALL OF OUR
MONOPRINT
WORK

ARTIST Carter A

During the war

After the outbreak of the Second World War, Douglas rejoined the RAF. He helped to develop the 'Big Wing' strategy, which sent large numbers of RAF fighters in mass formation against the Luftwaffe. The strategy was successful in bringing down significant numbers of enemy planes and it made such an impression on the Germans that they delayed the invasion of Britain.

By the summer of 1941, Douglas was the fifth most successful fighter ace in the RAF, having shot down twenty-three German aircraft. On 9th August, however, his run of successes came to an end when his Spitfire was shot down in northern France. After several escape attempts, Bader was sent to Colditz Castle as a prisoner of war. He was forced to wait there until the end of the war. On his release, he was promoted to group captain, leading a victory flypast of 300 aircraft over London.

After the war

He left the RAF in 1946 for a job with Shell Aircraft, where he stayed until 1969, before joining the Civil Aviation Authority. Having suffered a double disfigurement, Douglas became an inspiration to disabled and able-bodied alike by demonstrating the ability to "get on with your life." Post war found him working for Shell, playing golf and fundraising on behalf of many disabled charities. Douglas was honoured in 1976 with a knighthood for his contribution and work on behalf of the disabled community. He died of a heart attack on 5th September 1982, aged 72.

AUTHORS

Early life: Isobel S, Benjamin B, Harley R, Alfie F, James-Dean C.
Before the war: Rowan T, Letti B, Carter A, Isabelle-Bronte P, Samantha W, Maya K.
During the war: Kaila V, Poppy H, Sonny G, Amelia S, Ellie-Mai S.
After the war: Elizabeth S, Georgia H, Reuben R, Gabriella H, Isaac B, Marshall P.

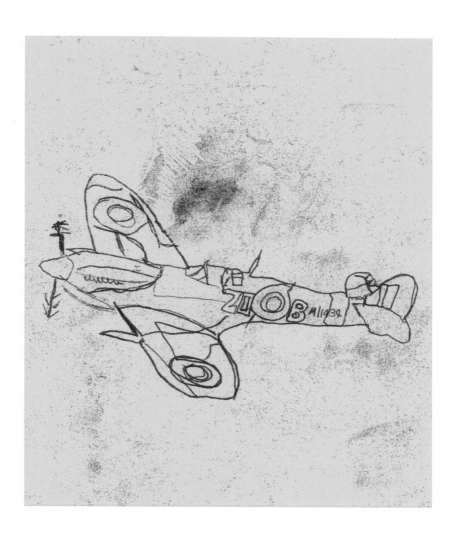

QUEEN
ELIZABETH II

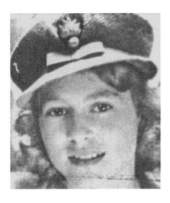

Early life

Queen Elizabeth II, who was christened Elizabeth Alexandra Mary Windsor, had an interesting childhood. She was born 21st April 1926 in Mayfair, London in a private hospital and was later followed by her sister Margaret. Interestingly, she was the first child of the Duke and Duchess of York who later became King George VI and Queen Elizabeth.

From a young age, Queen Elizabeth and Princess Margaret were homeschooled but later, they attended an all girls school with an assigned tutor. Throughout her education, she learned history, law and many languages. Sadly however, her peaceful childhood soon came to an end with the declaration of World War II.

Evacuation

On September 3rd 1939, World War II had just been declared when Queen Elizabeth was just 13 years old. Later, when the Blitz hit London, Buckingham Palace was bombed several times meaning Queen Elizabeth had to be evacuated. Originally, she was meant to be evacuated to Canada but she rejected the offer and went to Windsor Castle with her sister Margaret instead.

Queen Elizabeth (who was a princess at the time) sent her best wishes to evacuees all over the country. She said, "*Thousands of you in this country have had to leave your homes and be separated from your fathers and mothers. My sister Margaret Rose and I feel so much for you as we know from experience what it means to be away from those we love most of all.*"

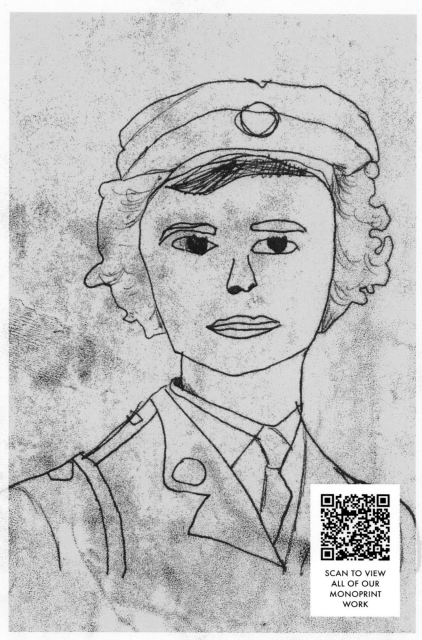

SCAN TO VIEW
ALL OF OUR
MONOPRINT
WORK

ARTIST Scarlett P

However, Queen Elizabeth was actually luckier than most evacuees as her parents stayed with them at Windsor Castle regularly.

During the war

During the war, Queen Elizabeth supported the war efforts through rationing and she was even photographed tending her allotments as part of the 'Dig for Victory' campaign. When Queen Elizabeth reached the age of 18, she wanted to support the war efforts even further so she joined the Auxiliary Territorial Service (ATS), which was the women's branch of the British Army. She was the first female in the Royal Family to join the armed forces. Surprisingly, Queen Elizabeth trained to be a driver and a mechanic and qualified on April 14th. She was a military first aid truck driver but certainly didn't mind being called an ambulance driver!
She was happy supporting the war and setting an example to others.

Queen Elizabeth maintained her war efforts until the day it ended, which is one of the many reasons the nation loved her.

End of the war

On 8th May 1945, World War II officially ended and is known as VE (Victory in Europe) Day. During the VE Day celebrations, Queen Elizabeth appeared on the balcony with her family six times. However, Elizabeth and Margaret wanted to celebrate with the crowds below and were given permission to leave Buckingham Palace to join in. When they were in the crowds, Queen Elizabeth was quite scared and covered her face with her hat to try and disguise herself.

After the war

After the war had ended, Queen Elizabeth's life didn't change that much because some aspects of the war were still in place such as rationing.

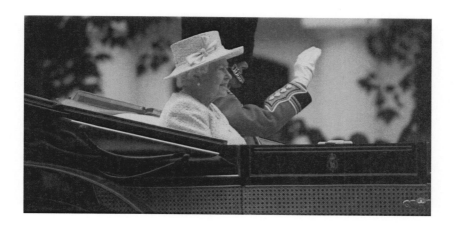

Queen Elizabeth was due to be married to Prince Phillip in 1952 but because of rationing, she wasn't able to buy a wedding dress. Instead, she had to save up her ration coupons to buy the material. Other people helped her by sending her coupons as a way of thanking her for what she had done for them. She also used some of the skills she had learned during World War II, such as driving, and she taught her own children to drive when they were old enough.

Queen Elizabeth supported her country during World War II but also for the rest of her life. She is still very much loved and remembered by her people for her efforts during World War II. We will always be grateful.

AUTHORS

Early life: Elise W, Kizzi B, Annis G.
Evacuation: Pandora A, Jacob M, Lucas T, Cody T-J.
During the war: Bodhi N, Jayden N, Thea W.
End of the war: Scarlett P, Mikey G.
After the war: Robyn H, Jack H.

SIR WINSTON
CHURCHILL

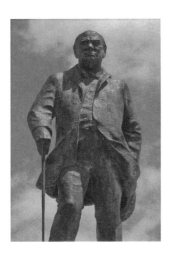

Early life

Winston Leonard Spencer Churchill was born on 30th November 1874 at Blenheim Palace in Oxfordshire. His parents were Randolph Churchill, son of the 7th Duke of Marlborough, and Jennie Jerome, an American woman. Churchill had a distant relationship with his parents and was mainly raised by his nanny, Elizabeth Everest. Despite achieving poor grades at boarding school, Churchill managed to get accepted at Harrow School before going on to join the British Army in 1893.

Life before the Second World War

After several years in the army, Churchill stood for election as a Member of Parliament. After initially losing, he was eventually elected as the Conservative Member of Parliament for Oldham in 1900 before moving to the Liberal Party in 1904. At the outbreak of the First World War, Churchill was serving as First Lord of the Admiralty. He oversaw the Gallipoli campaign, but it was a huge failure and he was forced to resign before travelling to the Western Front to fight. In 1919, shortly after the end of the war, he was appointed Secretary of State for Air and War. In this role he attended peace talks in Paris.

Becoming Prime Minister

In 1924, Churchill rejoined the Conservative Party. In the run up to the war, he constantly warned people of the rising threat of Nazi Germany but was often ignored. In 1938, Prime Minister Neville Chamberlain signed the

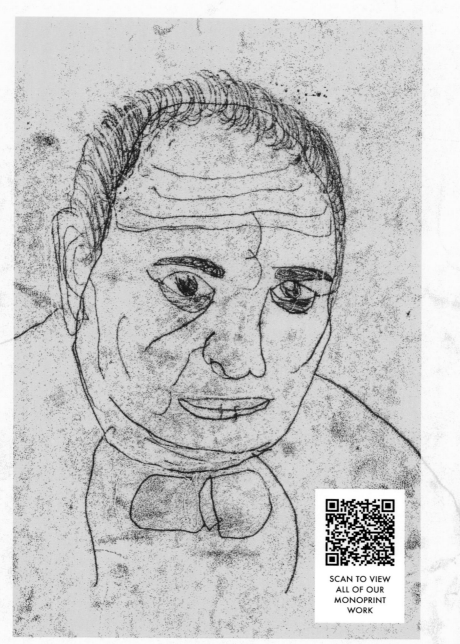

SCAN TO VIEW
ALL OF OUR
MONOPRINT
WORK

ARTIST Isla T

Munich Agreement with the Nazi leader, Adolf Hitler. Chamberlain declared that his appeasement of Hitler would lead to 'Peace for our time.'

Unfortunately, this peace was broken after Hitler invaded Poland in 1939, leaving them no choice but to declare war on Germany. In April 1940, Chamberlain was beginning to lose support in the House of Commons after months of German success. On 10th May 1940, Chamberlain resigned as Prime Minister and it became clear that only Churchill could unite and lead the nation.

Leadership during the Second World War

After becoming Prime Minister in 1940, Churchill remained in the job until the end of the war. In the dark, early days of World War II, Winston Churchill attacked with words instead of weapons. On the day Churchill became leader, Germany had already invaded Belgium, Luxembourg, the Netherlands and France. In his first speech to the House of Commons on 13th May 1940, Churchill warned of the difficult road ahead and offered nothing but 'blood, toil, tears and sweat.'

Churchill is well-known for giving inspirational speeches that helped to boost the spirits of the British people during the most difficult periods of the war. His 'victory at all costs' mentality and regular visits to those affected by the war helped to keep morale high across the nation. By May 1945, Germany had surrendered and the Japanese were close to being defeated.

Life after the Second World War

Following the end of the Second World War, Churchill's party lost the 1945 general election. In 1951, Churchill wanted revenge for his defeat in 1945 and became the Prime Minister for a second time after being re-elected in the general election.

By this point, Churchill was 77 years old and long past any normal retirement age. He was suffering from ill-health following several minor strokes and was forced to resign as Prime Minister in 1955.

Later life

Churchill remained a Member of Parliament until 1964 when he stood down at the general election. He spent most of his retirement at Chartwell or his London home in Hyde Park before sadly passing away on 24th January 1965, leaving behind his wife Clementine. He was honoured with a state funeral on 30th January and buried in Oxfordshire. Winston Churchill will be most remembered as a great wartime leader who guided his nation through its darkest hour.

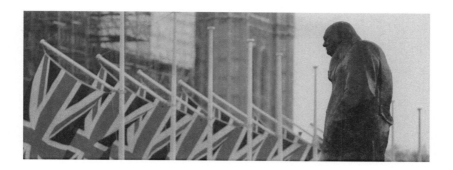

AUTHORS

Early life: Sophie K, Edward B, Ryla L, Esme P, Isla T, Stevie W.
Life before the Second World War: Grace Ha, Grace Hu, Emma C, Tobias M, Harry C.
Becoming Prime Minister: Andra V, Aoife H, Bobby C, Charlie T, Jason R.
Leadership during the Second World War: Naomi A, Erin P, Amelia-Rose S, Archie L.
Life after the Second World War: Jersey M, Millie P, Blake F, April-Grace F.
Later life: Lilly S, Emilea R, Joseph M, Ashton F, Chloe G, Sami-Jojo Y.

THE
BLITZ

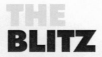

The terrifying bombs rapidly dropped on houses

Homes getting destroyed by thousands of dangerous, deadly bombs

Enemy aircraft droning up overheard making the air raid sirens wail
loudly in the sky

Brave and safe, people huddled together in the dull, dark shelters

Loud terrifying bombs dropped above them for hours at a time

It was an extremely terrifying experience!

The wardens came when it was safe for us to leave

Zooming planes had left for now

POETS

Kaila V, Rowan T, Gabriella H, James-Dean C, Marshall P.

Loud sirens ring out
German planes high in the sky
Cities bombed below
Jason R

Thousands of people dying from the bombs

Hitler invading Britain

Evacuation for the children to new countryside homes

Black out in Britain. Not a light to be seen

Lightning war for eight long months

Industrial areas targeted

The Blitz

Zooming air force in the dark sky. Sirens blaring

POETS

Luna S, Elliott W, Scarlett P, Victoria S.

Planes fly in the sky
The air raid siren is loud
Destruction is here!
Emma C

Planes were in the sky
Sirens screaming everywhere
Will this ever end?

Tobias M

Thousands of children evacuated to the countryside

Horrifying sirens wailing in the night sky. The Germans were coming!

Everyone running to the shelters when the air raid sirens go off

Big German aircraft flying over Britain, bombing the unsuspecting cities

Little children separated from their families

In London, Buckingham Palace was bombed with the King and Queen only just escaping

Thousands of people dying at the hands of Hitler and his German soldiers

Zooming planes flying overhead

POETS

Thea W, Pandora A, Macey F, Lucas G.

The Blitz was when German bombers attacked British cities

Hitler wanted to bomb us so Britain would stop fighting

Evacuees were evacuated to the countryside

Bombs were going off for eight long months

Lights out to keep everyone safe. Wardens checking for the blackouts

I had to go to the air raid shelter in the middle of the night

The Blitz

Zooming planes over head dropping bombs everywhere

POETS

Etta T, Bodhi N, Malakai S, Marcus G.

THE BLITZ

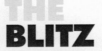

The children run to the air raid shelter
Here we stayed to keep us safe from the bombs
Evacuations from the big cities
Bombs are dangerous as they burn down the houses
Loving children terrified of the fire and explosions
Illuminated skies full of fog, smoke and fear
The children scared to find out if everyone is safe
Zipping from building to building

POETS

Isla T, Stevie W, Sami-Jojo Y, Chloe G.

Children were screaming
Exploding bombs were the worst
Planes drop from above
Charlie T

The children at school rushing to the underground shelter
Horrified children wondering if they would make it out alive
Evacuees being sent to the countryside
But most don't want to leave their parents
Lighting War was what the Germans would call it
In the first few days more than 1.5 million children are evacuated
Terrified children come out of the shelter, wondering what
remains in the destruction
Zooming German planes bombing the cities below

POETS

Jersey M, Lilly S, Edward B, Archie L.

People hugging tight
People scared of dropping bombs
Shelters protect us
Amber W

Blackouts keep us safe
Air raid wardens help people
Light must be covered

Florence S

Trains are leaving the big city

Homes of those are being bombed by the Germans

Evacuees are being moved to different houses

Bombs are hitting the homes below

Little children being taken from their parents

Icy winters leave a chill in the air

Thousands of people are losing their loved ones

Zap! The bomb has hit!

POETS

Aoife H, Bobby C, Amelia-Rose S.

The worried children sitting in the Morrison Shelter,

waiting for the siren to stop

Hopefully the children will be safe at school

Everyone's lives are at risk!

Bombs are striking everywhere in the big city

Luftwaffe planes drop bombs and many people are dying

It was an emotional time for everyone

The Germans target the city below

Zooming planes zip through the smoky sky

POETS

Naomi A, Erin P, April-Grace F, Joseph M.

THE BLITZ

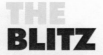

The Blitz

Horrifying history of World War II

Extreme explosions all around Britain

Bombs dropped all around

Lightning war was its name

Industrial areas targeted

Terrifying German planes overhead

Zooming over and releasing chaos

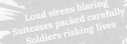

Loud sirens blaring
Suitcases packed carefully
Soldiers risking lives
Jack H

POETS

Samantha W, Marshall P, Georgia H.

The terrified people heard explosions across England

Houses bombed, people lost their lives

Enemy aircraft sending bombs towards our cities

Bellowing booms and bangs for days

Lightning war was it's translated name

It's black out time, this helped to keep us safe

Targets were our factories and ports

Zooming through the air, they came again and again

Soldiers here fighting
The air raid sirens go off
Growing our own food
Elliott W

POETS

Carter A, James-Dean C, Reuben R, Maya K.

Rushing out the house
Sirens screaming everywhere
Get to the shelter!
Blocking the lights out at night
War planes flying everywhere

Jersey M.

The Blitz was dangerous

Helpless people had their lives destroyed

Endless bombs dropped on us for days on end

Blackouts happened to keep us safe

Leave us alone - many cried out to the skies

Is war good or bad? It's hard to say

Terrified people ran for shelter

Zooming planes are here again

POETS

Elizabeth S, Alfie F, Kaila V.

Terrified people hiding in their Anderson Shelters

Hitler is causing this pain

Enemy aircraft drone overhead

Boom, Bang!

London was destroyed in the 'Lighting War'

Innocent people were killed

The pain and destruction needed to end

Zigzags in the sky, smoke rises from the cities

POETS

Rowan T, Sonny G, Gabriella H, Ellie-Mai S.

THE
WAR

The deadly frontline
Huge, smoky wasteland where battles took over
Every awful day, soldiers were injured or killed
Frightened and devastated at the war
Running into battle the soldiers went
One officer leading them a line at a time
No one dares go to No Man's Land
Tanks fired deadly shells
Luftwaffe flew over the huge, sludgy trenches
Injured soldiers carried safely away
No one had any happiness left inside of them
Everyone prayed for the war to end!

The smell of burning
Destroyed buildings everywhere
Sadness fills the air

Ashton F

POETS

Carter A, Elizabeth S, Maya K, Poppy H, Alfie F, Amelia S.

The bombs crashed on the fields
Horribly terrified soldiers
Everyone is running for shelter
Frightened men waiting in the trenches
Rapid bombs coming from the sky
Our poor soldiers, squealing for help
Not all men saw their families again
The battlefield was full of bodies
Lots of soldiers went to war but not all returned home
In debt we are to all
No man left behind on the battlefield
Everything was camouflaged

POETS

Reef R, Marnie-Rose E, Katie M, Reuben P.

People are dying
Soldiers marching to battle
To fight so we live
When we finish we will love
To make this alright tonight

Bobby C

Soldiers in the Blitz
They went off to fight for us
So we could be free

Kizzi B

Bombs loud like thunder
In battle many were lost
Gas clouds in the sky

Frankie K

We will survive but
This world is getting crazy
We have to be safe
Let's get weapons to survive
and win this horrible war

Andra V

The gloomy soldiers
Screaming from the fear of bombs
When will it all end?

Erin P, Lilly S, Harry C

War planes dropping bombs
Families are torn apart
Rubble everywhere
Innocent people dying
When will this destruction end?

Ryla L, Stevie W, Joseph M,
Sami-Jojo Y

Soldiers scream for help
Guns are firing like lightning
Soldiers are dying!

Florence S

FIELD WORK
EVACUEE DAY

As part of our hook week, the children were able to dress up as wartime evacuees! We then made our gas mask boxes and walked down to the nearby church. The children were able to experience what it may have felt like for a child during the 1940's who was about to be evacuated from their homes and into the countryside. The children were able to feel first hand what it may have been like to await selection into your new home as well as the feeling of potentially never seeing their parents again!

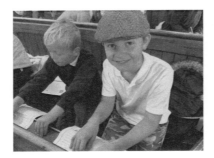
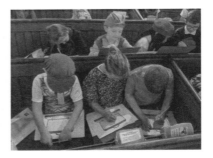

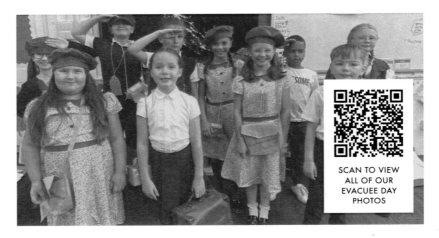

SCAN TO VIEW
ALL OF OUR
EVACUEE DAY
PHOTOS

Evacuees, gloomy and terrified, waited for their trains

Valuable children travelled to the countryside

A devastating day for everyone

Cities in England were destroyed by bombs

Underground shelters became a familiar safe place to hide

All the children were terrified and needed to be safe and thrive

The Germans started this

In the countryside, the children played happily in the open fields

Or learned calmly in their new schools

Not to return home until the end of the war, nobody thought this would

happen again

POETS

Ellie-Mai S, Isobel S, Sonny G, Benjamin B, Harley R.

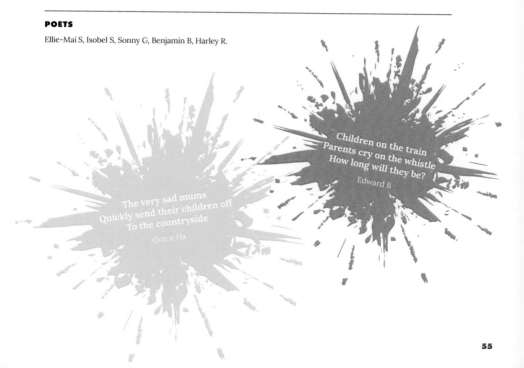

The very sad mums
Quickly send their children off
To the countryside

Grace Ha

Children on the train
Parents cry on the whistle
How long will they be?

Edward B

FIELD WORK
EVACUEE DAY

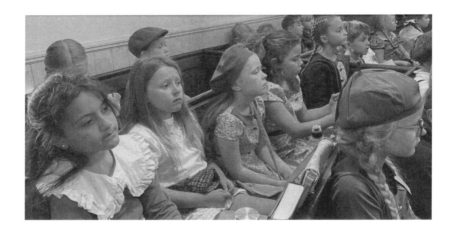

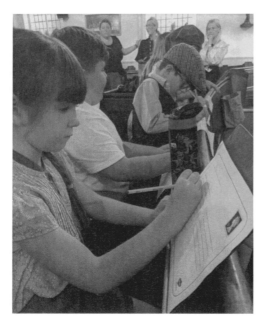

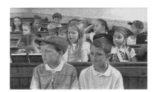

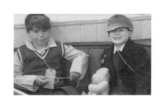

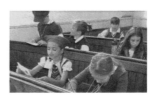

Evacuate the bombed, smoky city

Vast numbers of children are leaving

All homes destroyed

Children are going to safer towns

Unstoppable Germans started this horrible war

All aboard the evacuation train, going to a new life

Those evacuated feeling scared and alone

It happened for months on end

Only hope kept them going

Nobody knows if they will see their families again.

POETS

Layla R, Hollie H, Bobby T, Isla H, George H-B.

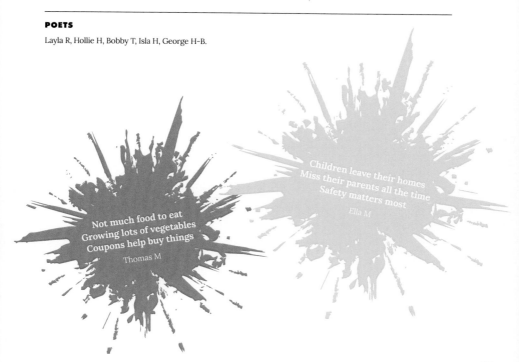

Not much food to eat
Growing lots of vegetables
Coupons help buy things

Thomas M

Children leave their homes
Miss their parents all the time
Safety matters most

Ella M

FIELD WORK
EDEN CAMP

During this expedition, we made a visit to Eden Camp to learn more about the Second World War. Eden Camp is a former prisoner of war camp that is located near Malton, North Yorkshire. The children were able to go in and out of the different huts with each hut having a different theme and 'experience' such as The Blitz, the Homefront and even a German U-boat!

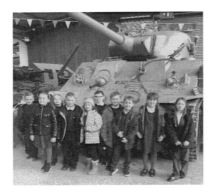
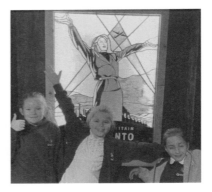

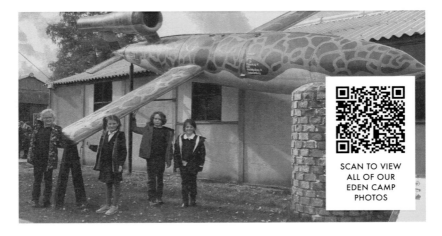

SCAN TO VIEW
ALL OF OUR
EDEN CAMP
PHOTOS

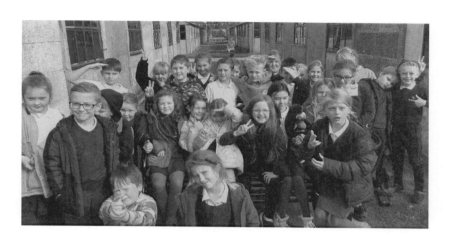

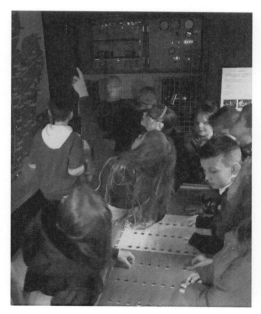

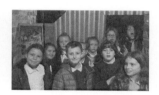

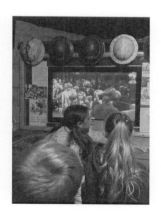

YEAR
THREE

During family learning, Y3 and Y4 invited parents and carers in to help us build our very own Anderson Shelters. We learnt all about The Blitz and how people would construct these shelters in their back gardens to keep them safe should they be bombed by the German planes. It is always a pleasure to welcome parents into school to immerse themselves within the expedition and see some of the amazing things that the children are learning about.

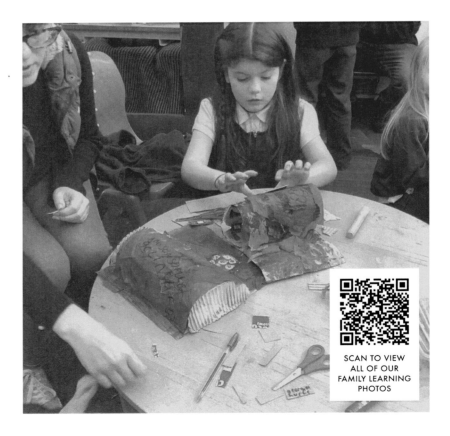

SCAN TO VIEW
ALL OF OUR
FAMILY LEARNING
PHOTOS

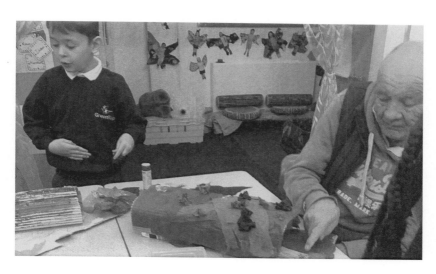

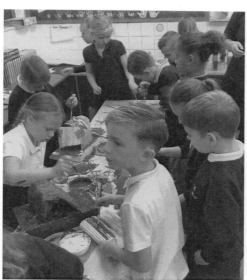

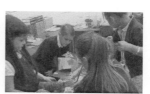

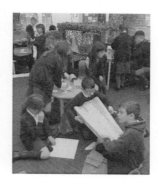

YEAR FOUR

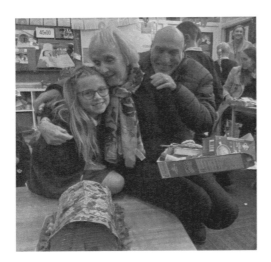

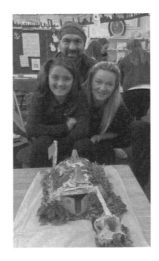

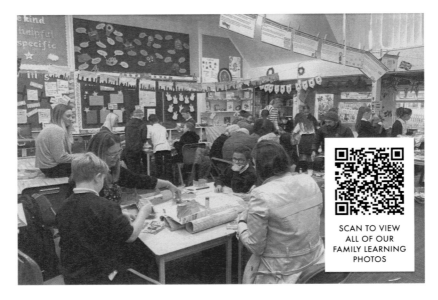

SCAN TO VIEW
ALL OF OUR
FAMILY LEARNING
PHOTOS

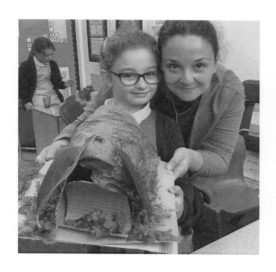
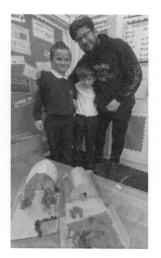
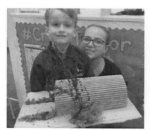
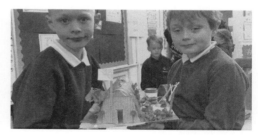
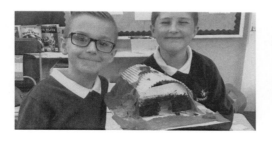
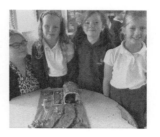

THORNE
REMEMBRANCE DAY SERVICE

On Sunday 13th November 2022, several Year 3 and 4 children from Green Top attended the local Remembrance Day Service at Thorne Park. The children placed down a wreath that had been created by the children on behalf of the school. Remembrance day is an important time of the year as we think about those brave men and women who sacrificed their lives and had to live through some of the worst times imaginable so that we could have a better future. Several examples of such stories are contained within this book.

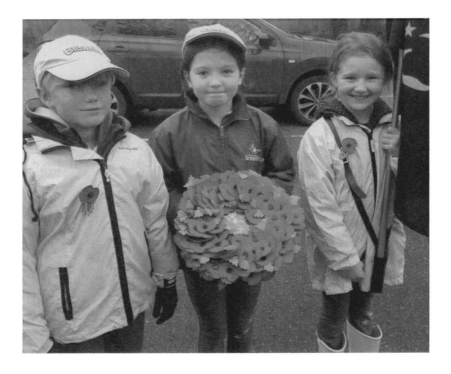

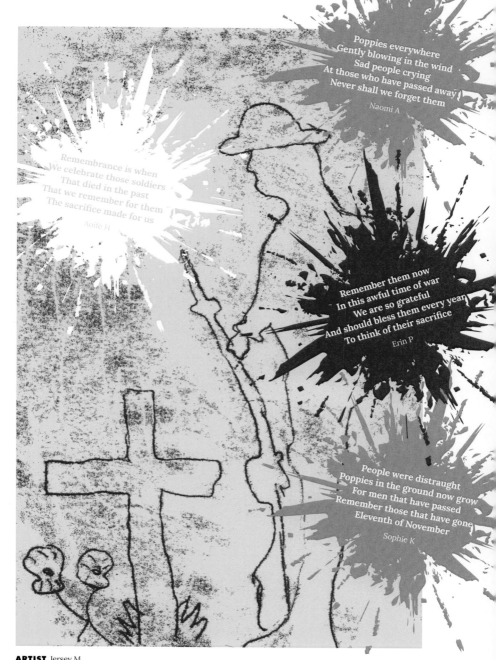

Poppies everywhere
Gently blowing in the wind
Sad people crying
At those who have passed away
Never shall we forget them

Naomi A

Remembrance is when
We celebrate those soldiers
That died in the past
That we remember for them
The sacrifice made for us

Aoife H

Remember them now
In this awful time of war
We are so grateful
And should bless them every year
To think of their sacrifice

Erin P

People were distraught
Poppies in the ground now grow
For men that have passed
Remember those that have gone
Eleventh of November

Sophie K

ARTIST Jersey M

THORNE
REMEMBRANCE DAY SERVICE

THEY SHALL GROW NOT OLD,
AS WE THAT ARE LEFT GROW OLD;
AGE SHALL NOT WEARY THEM,
NOR THE YEARS CONDEMN.
AT THE GOING DOWN OF THE
SUN AND IN THE MORNING
WE WILL REMEMBER THEM.

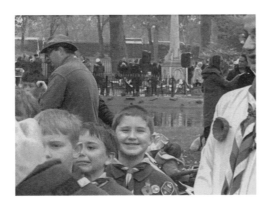

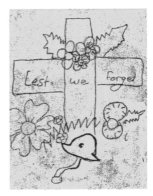

Rest they shall, in the bright Flanders fields

Everyone wears a beautiful, bright, red, poppy

Mournful and peaceful is their remembrance day

Everyone stops in silence, showing respect

Making beautiful wreaths

Bringing them to lay for the fallen soldiers

Remembering the soldiers who sacrificed their lives

And protected our country from Axis Powers

Never forgetting their gestures of kindness

Cenotaphs stand proud and tall, listing all of their names

Everyone remembers their glory days

Colourful poppies
Blood red poppies in the field
Remember soldiers
Jacob M

POETS

Samantha W, Isabelle-Bronte P, Georgia H, Letti B, Isaac B, Reuben R.

Bodies in the sun
Soldiers fighting to the death
Resting now at peace
Niah M

Remember the brave, heroic soldiers

Each person sacrificed their life

Magnificent soldiers fell

Eyes filled with tears

May they rest in peace

Be thankful for their service

Red poppies swaying

Amazing soldiers, saved our country

Never forgotten in our lifetime

Courageous until the end

Eleventh hour of the eleventh day of the eleventh month

All soldiers fighting
Poppies grow for dead soldiers
We remember them
Luna S

Poppies in the field
Soldiers died for our freedom
Silence in the field
Macey F

POETS

Isla D, Benjamin R-W, Lara S, Teddy A.

THORNE
REMEMBRANCE DAY
SERVICE

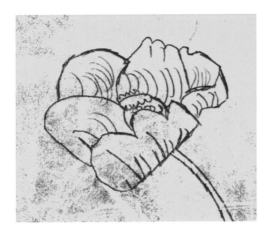

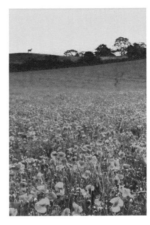

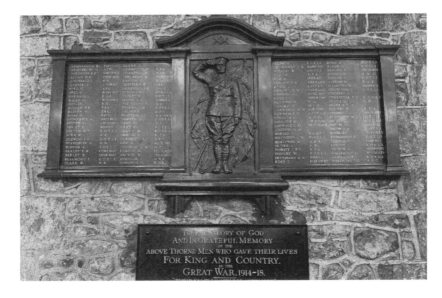

TO THE GLORY OF GOD
AND IN GRATEFUL MEMORY
OF THE
ABOVE THORNE MEN WHO GAVE THEIR LIVES
FOR KING AND COUNTRY.
IN THE
GREAT WAR, 1914~18.

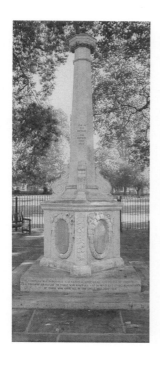

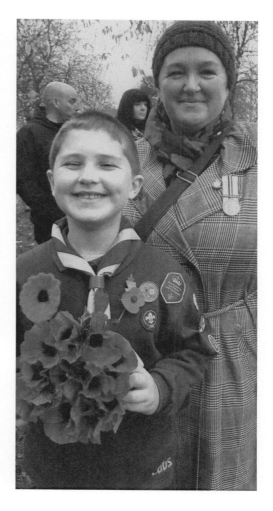

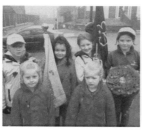

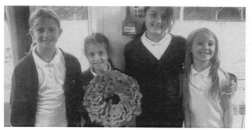

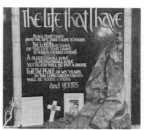

YEAR
THREE

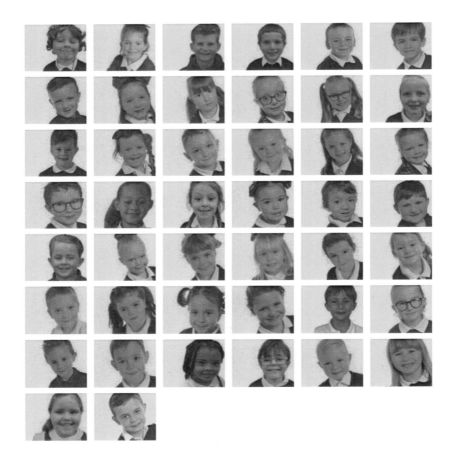

WE WILL NEVER FORGET